HEALTH CARE CAREERS IN 2 YEARS ™

JUMP-STARTING A CAREER IN

ULTRASOUND AND SONOGRAPHY

CORONA BREZINA

Rosen
YA ™

New York

Published in 2019 by The Rosen Publishing Group, Inc.
29 East 21st Street, New York, NY 10010

Library of Congress Cataloging-in-Publication Data

Names: Brezina, Corona, author.
Title: Jump-starting a career in ultrasound and sonography / Corona Brezina.
Description: First edition. | New York : Rosen YA, 2019. | Series: Health care careers in 2 years | Audience: Grades 7–12. | Includes bibliographical references and index.
Identifiers: LCCN 2018011693| ISBN 9781508185116 (library bound) | ISBN 9781508185109 (pbk.)
Subjects: LCSH: Ultrasonic imaging—Vocational guidance—Juvenile literature. | Diagnostic ultrasonic imaging—Vocational guidance—Juvenile literature.
Classification: LCC RC78.7.U4 B74 2019 | DDC 616.07/543023—dc23
LC record available at https://lccn.loc.gov/2018011693

Manufactured in the United States of America

CONTENTS

INTRODUCTION

For an expectant mother, the day of the midpregnancy ultrasound procedure brings feelings of excitement and anxiety. It represents a progress report on the pregnancy and the health of the developing fetus.

The ultrasound is performed by a diagnostic medical sonographer, who scans the mother's belly while observing the image on a monitor. To most observers, the screen appears to be an abstract jumble of different shades of gray. To the sonographer, however, the image conveys crucial medical information that she can decipher at a glance. (The field of sonography is largely dominated by women, and most sonographers who work in women's health specialties are women, according to labor force statistics compiled by the US Bureau of Labor Statistics [BLS] in January 2018.) She may point out the position and movement of the fetus on the screen to the mother. She'll monitor the baby's heart and determine whether it's a boy or a girl, if the position of the fetus will allow and the mother wishes to be told.

Many mothers remember this ultrasound procedure as their first baby picture. But for the sonographer, the most important aspects concern the health of the mother and fetus. The sonographer checks for abnormalities in the baby's anatomy and performs measurements that will

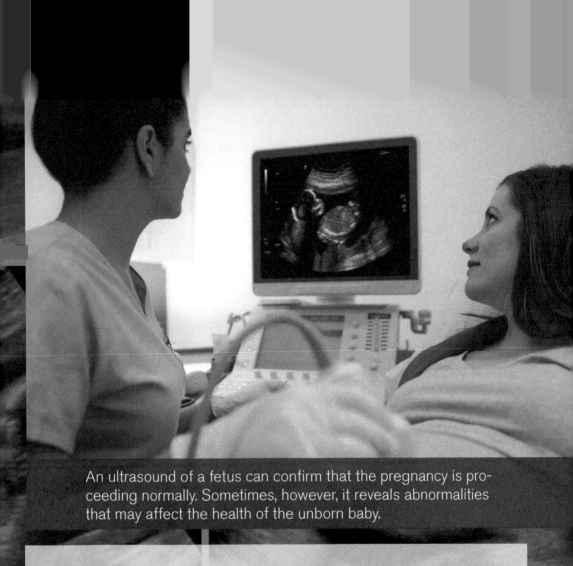

An ultrasound of a fetus can confirm that the pregnancy is proceeding normally. Sometimes, however, it reveals abnormalities that may affect the health of the unborn baby.

confirm the baby's growth and health. She will also confirm the health of the mother's reproductive organs.

Most mothers go home after the ultrasound thrilled to share the news that the baby is beautiful and healthy. In some cases, however, the sonographer may observe an abnormality that requires further scans or tests. If a serious condition is diagnosed, it may require treatment during pregnancy or intensive monitoring.

Although fetal ultrasounds are the best-known application of sonography, diagnostic medical sonographers perform many different types of ultrasound procedures on various areas of the body. Sonographers analyze abnormalities seen in ultrasound images to diagnose medical conditions. They often say that they have to act as detectives during the course of their work to figure out the correct diagnosis.

Sonography is a rewarding health care career that pays well after the completion of a two-year degree. Health care is an expanding sector of the economy, and sonography in particular is expected to experience job growth. The field of sonography is not for everyone—it requires a combination of people skills, technical ability, critical thinking, attention to detail, and mental and physical stamina. But many diagnostic medical sonographers consider it an exciting and fulfilling profession in which their work can play a pivotal role in a patient's diagnosis, treatment, and recovery.

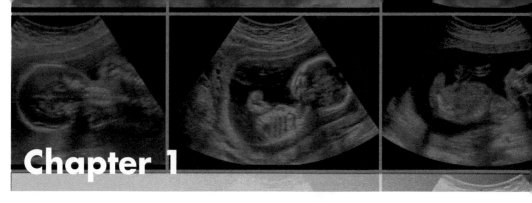

Chapter 1

SURVEYING THE FIELD

Diagnostic medical sonographers, also called ultrasonographers, ultrasound technicians, or ultrasound technologists, operate medical equipment that obtain images of a patient's body that are used for diagnosis. Sonography, sometimes called ultrasonography, is used to detect a broad range of different medical conditions.

Ultrasound has been utilized for various purposes for decades. Medical ultrasound imaging technology is based on the same principles that are applied in SONAR (SOund Navigation And Ranging) instruments. SONAR was employed by warships during World War II (1939–1945) to detect enemy submarines. After the war ended, scientists began investigating ways that ultrasound could be used to scan the human body. The first modern medical ultrasound equipment was introduced in the 1980s, taking advantage of advances in computing. Today, ultrasound is used in a variety of applications other than medicine, from motion sensors to industrial processing. A

Bats navigate and locate prey by echolocation, emitting high-pitched sounds that bounce off solid objects and are detected by their large, sensitive ears.

form of it even occurs in the natural world—bats avoid obstacles using echolocation, in which they bounce sound waves off of solid objects. Some marine mammals such as dolphins, porpoises, and toothed whales use echolocation, too.

What Is Sonography?

Sonographers use instruments that direct high-frequency sound waves into the body. The sound waves that are used for ultrasound procedures are too high in pitch for humans to detect them.

The most commonly used medical application of ultrasound is diagnostic ultrasound, which produces images of the body. The sound waves used in diagnostic ultrasound are produced by a probe called a transducer, which is connected to the ultrasound machine. Before beginning the procedure, the sonographer coats the area of the body being scanned with ultrasound gel, which ensures close contact between the transducer and the skin. (In some cases, the probe will instead be placed inside the body.) The sonographer rests the transducer on the skin and views the resulting image on a monitor throughout the procedure.

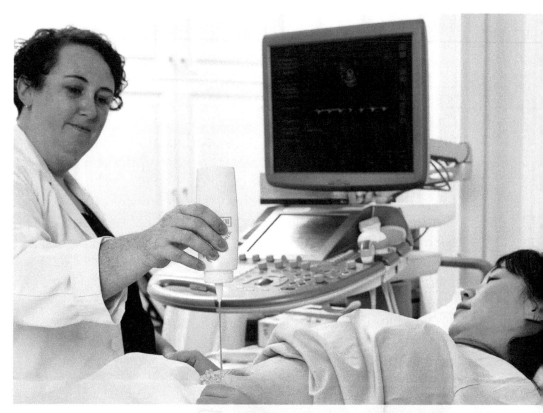

Ultrasound technicians apply ultrasound gel to the body to ensure a tight contact between the skin and the traducer, improving the transmission of sound waves.

The sound waves echo off the internal structures and are collected by the transducer as they reflect back. The returning sound waves are converted into images by the computer, which uses data such as the strength of the sound waves and the time it takes for them to reach the transducer. The result is the image that can be viewed on a screen in real time and recorded in forms such as still images or videos that may be printed out or stored as a digital file. The images produced by sonography are called sonograms, although they are sometimes referred to as ultrasounds as well.

Diagnostic ultrasound is best known for use in viewing the fetus of pregnant women, but it has many medical applications. Ultrasound scans can visualize blood vessels, the breast, eyes, the thyroid, the brain, organs and tissues in the abdomen, skin, and muscles. A procedure called an echocardiogram images the heart. Ophthalmic ultrasound is used to visualize the structures of the eye. Ultrasound can also be used to guide needles being inserted into a blood vessel or other part of the body. An advanced subtype of ultrasound, called functional ultrasound, can track changes occurring in an organ by measuring and imaging physical characteristics such as blood flow.

Traditional ultrasound scans are two-dimensional (2D), meaning that they visualize an image that appears flat. Three-dimensional (3D) ultrasound, which became available in the 1990s, gathers more data from different angles. The result is a more highly detailed image. Four-dimensional (4D) ultrasound is 3D ultrasound in motion, yielding a video rather than still images.

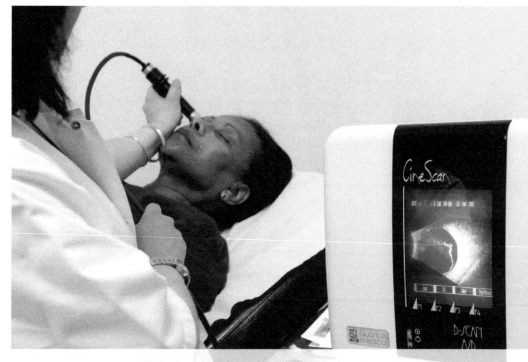

A focused ophthalmic ultrasound is performed on a patient's eye. The procedure is used to diagnose and monitor eye injuries or disorders such as foreign substances, cataracts, retinal detachments, and tumors.

A fourth type of ultrasound is Doppler ultrasound, which utilizes the Doppler effect—the apparent change in frequency of sound waves emitted by a moving object. Doppler ultrasound is used to scan moving structures in the body, especially blood flow. It is used in functional ultrasound, for example, and also to monitor the heart rate of a fetus. There are three types of Doppler ultrasound—color, power, and spectral—which each have advanced capabilities as well as limitations that make them beneficial for different kinds of situations.

Another medical application of ultrasound is therapeutic ultrasound, which is used to treat medical conditions. High-intensity sound waves can be applied to ablate (destroy) tissue, for example, or break apart kidney stones. Therapeutic ultrasound is generally a noninvasive procedure, requiring no cuts to the skin and leaving no scars.

Medical Imaging

Ultrasound is just one of many different tools used to obtain images and other information about a patient's anatomy and functioning. A related branch of health science is radiology, which involves X-rays and other instruments that employ ionizing radiation to scan the body. X-rays are the most commonly used form of diagnostic imaging. Radiologists also utilize MRI (magnetic resonance imaging), which uses a magnetic field rather than ionizing radiation.

There are advantages and disadvantages to both radiology and sonography procedures. In general, radiology procedures are expensive and time consuming. Ultrasound procedures are quick and less expensive, and they yield a faster diagnosis. X-rays and ultrasounds are each better suited to imaging particular parts of the body. X-rays are more effective at imaging bones—ultrasound does not penetrate bone and can only visualize the surface. X-rays are also better for scanning areas of the body that contain pockets of gas, which disrupt ultrasound waves. Ultrasound scans provide more detail about soft tissues than X-rays. In some cases, utilizing both ultrasound and X-ray scans of the same area can yield complementary results. Some technicians choose to receive training in both sonography and radiology.

Ultrasound has the advantage of being dynamic, meaning that the technologist can watch the real-time movement of body parts during the procedure. The images produced by ultrasound, however, are often not as clear or detailed as those obtained by X-rays, MRIs, and other forms of radiological imaging systems.

Some ultrasound devices are smaller and more portable than other types of imaging equipment. Ultrasound machines can sometimes be brought into the hospital room of a patient who is too fragile to move. An ultrasound can also be employed to perform a diagnostic scan quickly in an emergency room.

One frequently mentioned advantage of ultrasound over X-rays is the fact that ultrasound scans do not use ionizing radiation. Radiation exposure increases the risk of cancer. The levels of radiation used in imaging procedures are carefully controlled, however, and the US Food and Drug Administration (FDA) deems that the benefits of X-ray scans outweigh the health risks.

Radiation exposure is a much more significant concern for a developing fetus, however. That's why ultrasound is the standard imaging procedure used to monitor the progress of a pregnancy. A fetus is highly sensitive to harmful agents, such as radiation, some drugs, and infection. An abdominal X-ray performed during certain stages of pregnancy may increase chances of complications or damage to the fetus.

CAREERS IN RADIOLOGIC AND MRI TECHNOLOGY

Young adults who are interested in a career in medical imaging may be attracted to sonography as well as other types of imaging technology and have to pick a particular pathway. Those who choose radiologic technology or MRI technology operate X-ray machines, computed tomography (CT) machines, and mammography instruments to obtain clear images of the body's interior structures and systems. They also use MRI machines that can create full-body scans of patients and provide high levels of detail. Because radiologic technologists (also called radiographers) work with potentially harmful ionizing radiation, they need to take more safety precautions during their imaging procedures than sonographers.

An associate's degree can prepare a radiologic and MRI technologist for a career in the field, and the job outlook for the field is favorable, according to the BLS. An aging population in the United States is expected to require increased numbers of imaging procedures for diagnoses. Employment of radiologic technologists is projected to grow 12 percent from 2016 to 2026, much faster than the average for all occupations, and

employment of MRI technologists is expected to grow 14 percent. According to the BLS report on January 30, 2018, the median annual wage for radiologic technologists was $57,450 in 2016 and the median annual wage for MRI technologists was $68,420 in the same year.

Ultrasound has never been shown to harm a fetus, and it generally is regarded as safe. Nonetheless, it is a medical procedure, and the FDA and most doctors recommend that it should be performed only for diagnostic benefit—not to provide mothers-to-be with keepsake images of their unborn babies. If a sonogram reveals a cause for concern, a doctor may prescribe an MRI, which is also considered a safe diagnostic test for a fetus.

At the Workplace

Diagnostic sonography is a field with bright prospects for young people interested in pursuing a health care career. The health industry overall is expanding, partly because of an aging population in the United States that requires more medical services. Demand for noninvasive imaging procedures in particular is expected to increase.

In its *Occupational Outlook Handbook*, the BLS lists ultrasound and sonography job descriptions as "Diagnostic Medical Sonographers and Cardiovascular Technologists and Technicians, Including Vascular Technologists." According to the BLS January 2018 report, about 122,300 people were employed in these categories in 2016. Employment of diagnostic medical sonographers was projected to increase 23 percent over the next ten years, which is much faster than the average for all occupations. The employment of cardiovascular technologists and technicians, including vascular technologists, was projected to increase 10 percent over the next decade, which is faster than the average.

Hospitals are the largest employers in the field, employing 79 percent of cardiovascular technologists and technicians and 60 percent of diagnostic medical sonographers. Physicians also employ diagnostic medical sonographers and cardiovascular technologists and technicians in their offices, with many sonographers working for obstetricians—doctors who specialize in pregnancy, childbirth, and women's reproductive health. A small number of cardiovascular technologists and technicians and diagnostic medical sonographers work in outpatient care centers. About 11 percent of diagnostic medical sonographers work in medical and diagnostic laboratories. Some sonographers travel for the job, taking mobile ultrasound units to sites such as nursing homes, clinics, or even private homes that may require occasional ultrasound services.

Most diagnostic imaging workers hold full-time jobs. Employers may require working nights or weekends or

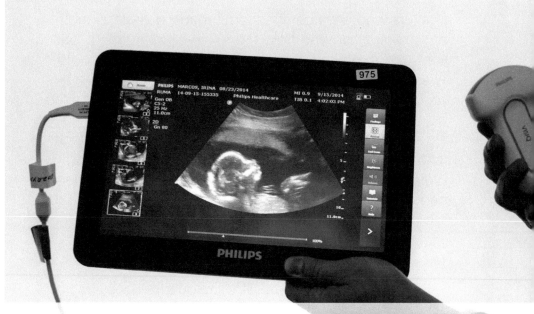

Portable ultrasound systems can enable sonographers to scan patients in a variety of different medical settings as well as for home health care treatment.

overnight shifts in hospitals or other facilities that are open twenty-four hours a day. Sonographers may be "on call" during some of their days off, meaning that they must go into work if needed.

According to the January 2018 BLS report, the median annual wage for diagnostic medical sonographers in 2016 was $69,650. The median annual wage for cardiovascular technologists and technicians in that year was $55,570. Entry-level sonographers, however, should expect to earn less than this amount. In addition, workers who earn certification through a professional organization or who hold higher levels of training, education, and experience are likely to be more highly paid. Average pay varies from one state to another as well— sonographers in California and Washington earned the highest annual average wages, for example, and the highest annual average wages for cardiovascular technologists and technicians were in Massachusetts and New Jersey. Detailed statistics on levels of employment and salary for every state can be found at the BLS website (https://www.bls.gov).

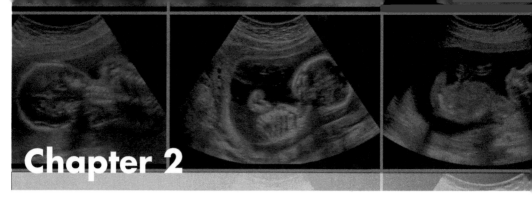

Chapter 2

DIAGNOSTIC MEDICAL SONOGRAPHERS

Diagnostic medical sonography is a challenging and rewarding health care career field. Patients are often stressed and nervous when they arrive for an ultrasound procedure. A sonographer's work helps resolve some of their medical questions. An expectant mother may see the first images of her fetus. A patient experiencing abdominal pain may receive a diagnosis that will help determine treatment options. Sonography is an in-demand field that involves interacting with a variety of different people through the course of the workday and requires a combination of technical, interpersonal, and critical-thinking skills.

Sonography is categorized as a career in allied health, which describes the wide range of health care fields other than medicine and nursing. Allied health professionals perform many different types of services related to diagnosing, treating, and preventing disease. Like most allied health workers, sonographers work alongside doctors and nurses, performing a specialized service that is essential to patient care.

A Day on the Job for a Sonographer

Sonography is a hands-on job. Before the patient arrives for a procedure, the sonographer selects and sets up the appropriate equipment. When the patient comes in, the sonographer may take a medical history. The sonographer may have already discussed the case with the referring physician as well. In some cases, the patient will have been given instructions on how to prepare for the procedure, such as not eating for a certain amount of time beforehand. The sonographer will explain the procedure and answer any of the patient's questions.

Sonographers interact with patients during the entire procedure. They must be prepared to deal with any type of patient, including people with physical or mental disabilities. They may need to calm worried patients or remain professionally courteous with patients who are sick and cranky.

The sonographer then positions the patient, who generally lies face up on an examination table, and ensures that he or she is comfortable. This task may involve helping to lift a patient in a wheelchair or draping the hospital gown around the part of the body being scanned. The sonographer adjusts the equipment, if necessary, and applies the gel.

The sonographer begins the procedure by applying the transducer to the skin and slowly moving it back and forth to obtain a good image of the area of interest. He or she watches the monitor and adjusts the controls to capture good-quality images that will show satisfactory detail for a conclusive diagnosis. Sonographers are highly knowledgeable about the part of the

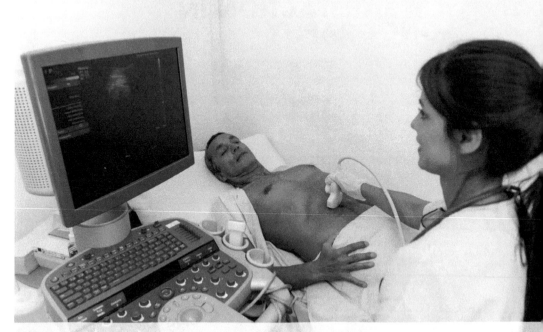

A sonographer must be familiar with the structures of the body in the area being scanned. An abdominal ultrasound, for example, makes scans of organs such as the kidneys and liver.

body being scanned and are able to identify healthy and diseased areas. If the sonographer views unexpected results, he or she may adjust the scope of the planned procedure. The images are then recorded, as videos or stills, or both. An ultrasound procedure usually takes less than half an hour, although some scans may take longer.

After the procedure is completed, the sonographer cleans off the gel or offers the patient tissue to clean himself or herself off. He or she may ask the patient to

JOB SATISFACTION IN SONOGRAPHY

Practicing sonographers shared some of their thoughts about the career on the website for the American Registry for Diagnostic Medical Sonography, Inc.:

This is a career that tests your expertise daily and changes from moment to moment ... It also affords you the opportunity to grow within the field, by acquiring certification in multiple specialties, so that you can broaden or focus your expertise, as desired.

A successful sonographer is someone who has an independent personality, who is bright, has strength of character and a strong ethical background. It is also important to have a spontaneous personality and enjoy working with and dealing with people.

An ultrasound professional must be compassionate, flexible and detail-oriented! We are making life-altering decisions that impact patient management, so we must be prepared both academically and emotionally to provide careful and thoughtful care. Professionally, a sonographer needs to have the academic background and clinical expertise to function in a fast-paced and caring environment.

wait until the images have been double-checked for quality and coverage of the areas needed for diagnosis.

Sonographers are responsible for providing a technical interpretation of the images for the physician. The sonographer summarizes the test findings in a report. He or she makes notes of the types of images taken and the content. During a routine day at work, sonographers perform numerous scans and interpret the results.

Activities and Responsibilities

A job as a diagnostic medical sonographer involves more than the time spent operating the ultrasound machine. The equipment is central to the job, however. Sonographers maintain the machines, calibrating them and checking for malfunctions. It's also important for sonographers to keep up with the latest advances in technology in the field.

Sonographers will have to learn to operate new and upgraded equipment

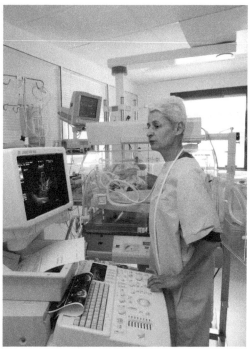

A sonographer uses Doppler ultrasound to image the blood flow in the brain of an infant. Ultrasounds of the head are particularly important in evaluating premature babies.

and software, and they may help make decisions about purchasing new equipment.

Like all health care professionals, diagnostic medical sonographers are responsible for documenting their work and updating patient records. In smaller facilities without a large administrative support staff, sonographers may be responsible for more paperwork. Sonographers must also be savvy about navigating hospital bureaucracy. They work under supervisors, doctors from various departments who order the tests, and radiologists—the doctors who diagnose the images taken by the sonographer. Scheduling can also be complicated for sonographers. A sonographer may have to deal with a heavy workload, cancellations, prioritizing urgent cases, rotating shifts, and staying late to finish writing up a report.

A sonographer's daily routine could also involve miscellaneous odd jobs, such as ordering and stocking medical supplies for the department. Periodically, a sonographer might attend workshops or conferences to learn about cutting-edge technology and the latest trends in the industry.

One of the diagnostic medical sonographer's greatest responsibilities involves the "diagnostic" description in the job title. A sonographer's job involves using professional skills, judgment, and knowledge to a greater extent than is required in other imaging specialties. A sonographer must approach each procedure on a case-by-case basis. His or her observations during the scan may alter the course of the procedure if the sonographer decides that additional images may be necessary to provide enough information for a diagnosis. The sonographer might change the settings on the equipment, scan a larger area than intended, or provide detailed images of an abnormality. A sonographer will contact the physician immediately if he or she identifies a potentially life-threatening condition.

A sonographer's technique is also a factor in acquiring high-quality images. A sonographer may encounter, for example, an abnormality that is concealed by surrounding tissue or subtle shading differences that indicate the early stages of a disease. A skilled sonographer knows the best way to maneuver the transducer to capture good images under various circumstances or recognize when an abnormality might appear in more detail if the patient is in motion during the scan.

The sonographer's responsibilities generally do not include notifying the patient of findings, however, although laws and policies vary among different states and health care facilities. A sonographer might describe what is being displayed on the monitor during a scan, but he or she does not offer interpretation of the images. If a patient asks the sonographer whether there's any cause for concern, the sonographer will probably reply that the health care provider will contact him or her with the results of the procedure.

Key Skills and Traits

As described previously, a career as a diagnostic medical sonographer requires technical and mechanical aptitude in operating specialized equipment. A sonographer must also have a solid understanding of anatomy and physiology. Exceptional powers of observation are necessary for distinguishing different gray

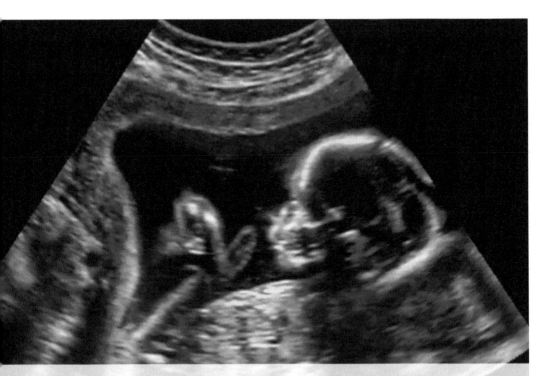

An experienced sonographer is familiar with the anatomy of a fetus. He or she will be able to determine the gender and identify possible defects or complications.

tones or color combinations on both the monitor and in recorded images. Hand-eye coordination is also essential to manipulate the transducer to yield the desired images on the monitor.

The job may also require a degree of physical strength and stamina. Sonographers spend much of their day on their feet, and they may have to move patients and push heavy equipment. Sonographers experience a high rate of musculoskeletal strain injuries from the job, especially in the neck, shoulders, wrist, hands or fingers, and back. It's a good idea for young people interested in a sonography career to pay close attention to recommendations on safety practices during education and training. In addition, most sonographers work in health care settings, where they're particularly likely to be exposed to infectious diseases.

Good communication skills—written and verbal—are essential for a sonographer. A sonographer must be able to put patients at ease. He or she must explain technical procedures clearly and be able to answer the patient's questions in accessible language—sonographers need to be good listeners as well. The sonographer must also be confident using medical terminology, which is essential to understanding and carrying out the physician's orders.

An enthusiasm for solving problems and an ability to think critically are also important characteristics for a sonographer. It may take some effort to acquire good quality images or reach a diagnosis. Experienced sonographers often say that they enjoy the challenge of figuring out the solution that explains a patient's symptoms. Sonography requires mental as well as physical stamina—sonographers cannot allow their minds to wander during a procedure.

A sonographer must have excellent people skills. The job requires one to spend much of the workday around patients and other hospital personnel. A sonographer should be willing to take direction from and collaborate with a variety of medical personnel, including doctors, nurses, supervisors, administrators, and other sonographers. A sonographer should demonstrate empathy and

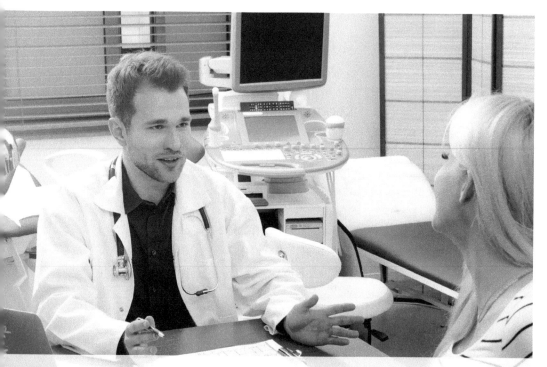

A sonographer must have great communication skills that will enable him or her to reassure nervous patients and explain the details of the procedure clearly.

patience in dealing with patients, but professional detachment is also necessary to evaluate abnormalities without allowing emotions to interfere with the assessment.

Sonographers should be motivated by a desire to help people, not by a desire to receive praise and gratitude for every diagnosis. Patients often don't recognize a sonographer's level of skill and the important role they play in determining a diagnosis. While many patients are sincerely appreciative, a sonographer should get satisfaction from doing the job well.

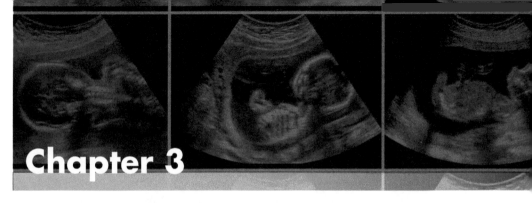

Chapter 3

SPECIALIZATIONS IN ULTRASOUND AND SONOGRAPHY

Many diagnostic medical sonographers specialize in a particular area of imaging. The BLS highlights obstetric and gynecologic sonographers, breast sonographers, abdominal sonographers, musculoskeletal sonographers, pediatric sonographers, cardiac sonographers, and vascular technologists.

In addition to these common specialties, some sonographers specialize in rarer areas. Neurosonographers examine the structure of the brain and the nervous system. They generally use a transcranial Doppler machine that monitors the speed of blood flow in vessels of the brain. Neurosonographers detect conditions that affect the brain, such as stroke, brain trauma, Alzheimer's disease, brain tumors, and epilepsy. The spinal cord is also a part of the nervous system, and neurosonographers can also identify disorders such as multiple sclerosis and paralysis. Some neurosonographers choose the subspecialty of neonatal

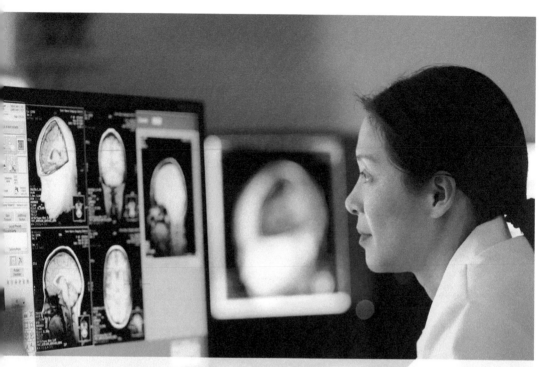

Neurologists—doctors who treat disorders related to the brain, spinal cord, and nervous system—utilize ultrasound images as well as other tests such as magnetic resonance imaging (MRI) scans.

neurosonography, which deals with newborn infants, especially high-risk infants, such as those born premature. They may detect disorders such as spina bifida, Down syndrome, and cerebral palsy.

Ophthalmologic sonographers image the eye, including the muscles attached to the eye. An ultrasound scan can provide information on the interior of the eye when it has become clouded, such as by cataracts. Different types of scans can reveal different information. One scan may image the structures of the eye, for example, while another examines blood flow.

Obstetric and Gynecologic Sonographers (OB-GYN)

Obstetric and gynecologic (OB-GYN) sonographers specialize in imaging the female reproductive system. Many pregnant women receive obstetric ultrasounds to track the baby's growth and health. The image shows the developing fetus as well as the woman's reproductive organs. A woman generally has an ultrasound

Three-dimensional (3D) ultrasound images show a fetus at the age of twenty-six weeks. Obstetricians may order a 3D ultrasound test if they are concerned about possible complications.

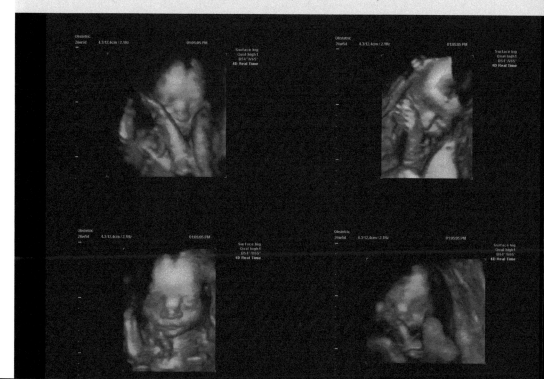

early in the pregnancy, to establish a delivery due date, and a second at about eighteen weeks to check the progress of the pregnancy. If the mother or fetus have any health issues, there may be additional ultrasounds performed.

The midpregnancy ultrasound is the occasion at which the mother learns the sex of the baby, if she chooses to be told. The sonographer establishes the size of the fetus, assesses the overall health, and visualizes the structures of the fetus to look for any abnormalities. He or she also checks the position and status of the reproductive organs around the fetus. The sonographer may also perform a Doppler ultrasound to assess the blood flow. If there is any cause for concern, the obstetrician may order a 3D ultrasound, a 4D ultrasound, or a transvaginal ultrasound, in which the transducer is inserted into the vagina. The obstetrician may also request follow-up tests or procedures in addition to ultrasound scans.

Some sonographers specialize in both obstetric and gynecologic sonography while others focus on either one or the other. Gynecology is the branch of health care dealing with women who are not pregnant, especially regarding their reproductive health. Gynecologic ultrasound procedures scan for medical conditions that affect the reproductive organs.

Breast Sonographers

Breast sonographers specialize in taking images of a patient's breast tissue. Sonography can confirm the

MIDWIFE SONOGRAPHY

A midwife is a medical professional who provides medical, emotional, and practical support to a woman throughout pregnancy and childbirth. Some women choose to turn to a midwife rather than a physician for prenatal care and attendance at birth. Many prospective mothers perceive midwives' approach to be more natural, and midwives are less likely than physicians to suggest medical intervention during the course of a healthy, low-risk pregnancy and childbirth.

Midwifery is an old, traditional profession that existed before the emergence of the modern medical system. Modern midwives, however, are thoroughly trained and educated health practitioners. Most of the midwives in the United States are certified nurse-midwives who consult with an obstetrician if medical intervention is necessary. The tools available to midwives include ultrasound—in 2017, the American Registry for Diagnostic Medical Sonography (ARDMS), which offers sonography credentials, introduced a midwife sonography certification. To be eligible, a candidate must hold midwife certification and complete a certain number of hours of training in OB-GYN ultrasound. Certification requires passing an exam and demonstrating successful practical experience using sonography.

presence of cysts and tumors that may have been detected by the patient, the physician, or a mammogram—an X-ray screening of the breast. Ultrasound procedures do not replace mammography, but they are valuable for obtaining additional information about an abnormality. Ultrasound imaging can differentiate between a fluid-filled cyst and a solid tumor, for example, and identify some tumors that are not detected by a mammogram.

A doctor may order a biopsy of a lump found in the breast. During the procedure, in which a needle is inserted to take a sample, ultrasound may be used to monitor the area around the lump.

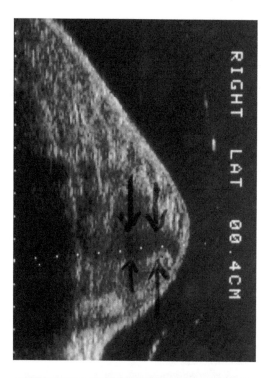

An ultrasound scan of a woman's breast shows a cancerous tumor. A doctor may order a breast ultrasound to learn more about a lump or other abnormalities.

Abdominal Sonographers

Abdominal sonographers specialize in imaging a patient's upper abdominal cavity and nearby organs, such as the liver, gallbladder, pancreas, kidneys, spleen, urinary bladder, and blood vessels. A patient may be referred for an abdominal ultrasound for reasons such as pain or swelling, abnormal results from a lab test, or kidney or gallbladder stones. Doppler ultrasound may be used to examine blood flow or abnormalities in the vessels. The results from an abdominal ultrasound can be used to diagnose a wide variety of conditions, from cirrhosis of the liver to blood clots in a vessel. Abdominal ultrasound can also be used to help place the needle during biopsies or other procedures requiring ultrasound guidance, such as draining fluid.

Musculoskeletal Sonographers

Musculoskeletal sonographers specialize in imaging muscles, soft tissue, ligaments, tendons, and joints. Ultrasound is not effective in penetrating bone, but it is well-suited for showing fine details of injuries to small parts such as tendons or ligaments in the hands. It can also reveal foreign bodies in soft tissue, such as wood, glass, or metal slivers. A musculoskeletal sonographer may diagnose injuries such as sprains, strains, or tears, inflammation, tumors, or conditions such as carpal tunnel syndrome or hernias. Musculoskeletal sonographers may scan children for conditions such as soft tissue masses, neck muscle abnormalities, or a dislocated hip in infants. Ultrasound can also be used to guide injections of medications and other treatments.

Pediatric Sonographers

Pediatric sonographers specialize in imaging children and infants. Performing procedures on children isn't equivalent to imaging a smaller version of an adult—children have different proportions and physiology. A pediatric sonographer is trained in which equipment and techniques to use for scanning children's anatomy and in identifying medical conditions likely to be diagnosed in children. Ultrasound is useful in evaluating appendicitis, for example, which is a common surgical emergency in children. Pediatric sonographers also image medical conditions associated with premature births or birth defects.

A pediatric sonographer must have patience and be skilled at soothing or distracting children or infants to get them to lie still for the procedure. A parent typically accompanies a child in the examination room during the imaging procedure.

Cardiovascular Sonography

Two specializations in sonography are often associated with the unit of a hospital dealing with heart and vascular health or a cardiologist's office. They generally work alongside other cardiology technologists, such as electro-cardiogram (EKG) technicians.

CARDIAC SONOGRAPHERS (ECHOCARDIOGRAPHERS)

Cardiac sonographers, also called echocardiographers, specialize in imaging the heart, its chambers, valves, and vessels. The test, called an echocardiogram, visualizes the size and shape of the heart as well as its functioning. Echocardiograms can be used to diagnose heart conditions such as valve problems, congestive heart failure, and heart defects. They can also help assess damage caused by a heart attack.

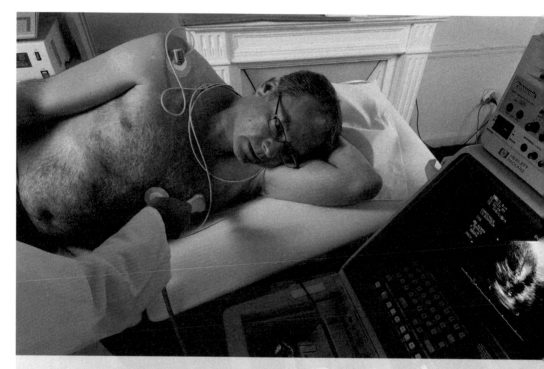

A sonographer performs an echocardiogram to make images of the structures of the heart, monitor blood flow, and evaluate overall heart health.

The standard type of echocardiogram is a transthoracic echocardiogram, in which the echocardiographer scans the area of the chest and abdomen over the heart. It may be necessary for the patient to be injected with a contrast agent—a liquid injected into the blood that will improve the image quality. A Doppler echocardiogram examines the flow of blood through the heart and vessels. A stress echocardiogram observes the effects of physical activity on the heart. The patient undergoes an echocardiogram before and after physical exercise, and the results are compared. A transesophageal echocardiogram is an invasive procedure in which the transducer is guided through a tube down the esophagus, which connects the mouth to the stomach.

There are three subspecialties within cardiac sonography. Adult echocardiographers scan the adult heart for conditions such as coronary artery disease. Pediatric echocardiographers scan the hearts of children for conditions such as congenital heart disease, or a defect that has been present since birth. Fetal echocardiographers perform scans on the fetus of a pregnant woman to assess potential abnormalities in the developing heart.

VASCULAR TECHNOLOGISTS (VASCULAR SONOGRAPHERS)

Vascular technologists, also called vascular sonographers, specialize in imaging the blood vessels of the circulatory system. Vascular sonography images help physicians diagnose disorders affecting blood flow, assess the success of treatments such as coronary bypass surgery, and decide whether a patient might be a good candidate for a surgical procedure. A vascular ultrasound can monitor blood flow throughout the abdomen, limbs, and neck, and to tissues and organs, including the brain. Vascular technologists diagnose issues such as blockages, abnormalities, clots, and aneurysms, which are enlarged arteries. Doppler sonography can be used to evaluate blood flow. Pediatric vascular imaging is helpful in placing needles into children's veins or arteries, which are smaller than an adult's blood vessels.

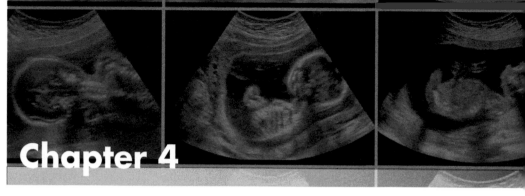

Chapter 4

GETTING A SONOGRAPHY EDUCATION

At the workplace, a diagnostic medical sonographer performs imaging procedures leading to diagnoses that can change the course of a patient's life. It's a big responsibility, and sonography education and training programs fully prepare students in every aspect of the job. Sonography programs are thorough and rigorous. Students learn technical skills (such as operating the instruments on sonography equipment), anatomy, patient care, and medical ethics. They spend time in the classroom and in health care facilities learning to master clinical responsibilities. Most sonographers hold an associate's degree, making sonography a relatively affordable career option that can quickly lead to a well-paying job.

High School

Laying a foundation for becoming a great sonographer can start with sound academic choices and hard work in high school. You should establish a solid work ethic, good study habits, and a lifelong love of learning.

Anyone pursuing a career in health care should take a wide range of science and math classes in high school. Knowledge of biology is fundamental in the field, and chemistry and physics are also central to sonography. You should also sign up for courses in anatomy, physiology, and health if your school offers them. An expertise in cutting-edge technology is essential for a sonographer, so you should take computer classes as well. Because good written and verbal communication skills are necessary for the job, take courses in English.

Sonography training isn't offered in high-school level programs, but some vocational-technical (vo-tech) centers offer training for jobs in health care that serve as good

High school science classes can provide a sound background for a career in sonography, which requires solid knowledge of chemistry, physics, and several branches of biology.

preparation for a job in sonography. Examples include a general course in health care or specific health care jobs such as medical assistant or nursing aide. Some vo-tech institutions may partner with colleges, universities, or hospitals, too. A high school student may be able to earn college credit toward a degree or gain clinical experience in a hospital setting in addition to classroom study. These types of programs would give you a hands-on opportunity to learn practical skills in a health care setting.

Extracurricular activities, volunteer work, and summer jobs can also provide good experience that will look good on your résumé for a future job in health care. Sign up for science fairs or any clubs related to technology.

By volunteering in a hospital, students can experience the daily routines involved in providing health care and decide whether they'd want to work in a medical setting.

Volunteer in a local health care facility—if there is an ultrasound department, ask if they ever give demonstrations. Take a summer job related to health care or customer service. Customer service skills can be a valuable asset in a sonography job, which requires positive interactions with a variety of patients and health care staff throughout the day.

Experts in the field suggest that a student interested in pursuing a sonography career "job shadow" a sonographer—observe a sonographer's daily duties on the job during a shift. You can learn about job shadowing opportunities by contacting medical facilities or a sonography educational institution in your region.

Sonography Education and Training

Sonography programs are offered at four-year schools that award a bachelor's degree, two-year programs that award an associate's degree, and one-year certificate programs that are often affiliated with teaching hospitals. Generally, only experienced health care professionals who are changing careers within the field are eligible for certificate programs. Radiological technologists, for example, might choose to improve their job prospects by acquiring sonography certification.

Most sonographers receive their education and training through a two-year education and training program. They are usually offered at community and technical colleges, but some colleges and universities also offer two-year programs. If you are considering your options for a diagnostic medical sonography program, research the institution before you apply. Because sonography is a high-tech field, look for a school with state-of-the-art equipment. If you're interested in studying a particular specialty, check whether it offers training in that area. Read the program description to check whether it partners with health care facilities to provide students with opportunities for clinical rotations. Find out when you can attend an information session about the program.

Reputable programs are accredited by accrediting agencies such as the Commission on Accreditation of Allied Health Education Programs (CAAHEP). If you're uncertain whether a sonography program is properly accredited, you can check the CAAHEP website for a list of certified programs by state along with contact information. Don't underestimate the importance of accreditation, which guarantees the professional standards of educational programs. Moreover, certification organizations, such as the ARDMS, generally require that applicants complete an accredited educational program to be eligible for certification. Many employers prefer to hire job candidates who hold certification. Therefore, your choice of an educational program can potentially impact your long-term career arc.

Once you've narrowed down your preferred educational programs, don't delay submitting your application. Admission can be competitive for high-quality sonography programs, and enrollment is often limited. The application process may include an interview in which the applicant discusses why he or she wants to become a sonographer and career expectations. Look into sources of financial aid as well. Scholarships, grants, and loans are available from federal and state programs, nonprofit organizations, and educational institutions. Some professional and health

A college financial department can offer help and recommendations in applying for financial aid, which can be a complicated and difficult process.

related organizations offer private scholarships to students studying sonography.

Most sonography programs are full-time and require a significant time commitment—programs often request that students don't hold a job so that they can fully concentrate on their education. Coursework for a sonography program includes math, science, information technology, anatomy, physiology, patient care, psychology, ethics, law, medical terminology, instrumentation, and the principles of sonography. Some classes may be available

TAKING THE TEST

Candidates who wish to obtain credentials with organizations such as ARDMS, Cardiovascular Crediting International (CCI), or American Registry of Radiologic Technologists (ARRT) must pass a test to qualify. Certification examinations are generally timed tests lasting a minimum of several hours that are taken on a computer at a testing center. Most examinations can be scheduled at any time, but some are offered only during specific windows throughout the year.

You should familiarize yourself with the length and format of the test ahead of time. Most examinations consist mostly of multiple choice questions, but other types of assessment may be included, too. The Sonography Principles and Instrumentation (SPI) administered by ARDMS, for example, incorporates a simulated console that tests the student's understanding of the ultrasound equipment.

Certifying organizations will include preparation advice on their websites, including an overview of the content covered by the examination. They may also

(continued on the next page)

(continued from the previous page)

provide information on study materials and practice tests or self-assessments.

On exam day, you should plan to arrive early. Make sure you have appropriate identification and check the exam center's rules ahead of time.

online. The programs generally involve extensive clinical coursework in hospitals, clinics, and other medical facilities as well. Students will gain experience in a range of different health care settings. In many programs, students focus on a particular specialty, such as OB-GYN, echocardiography, or vascular, as they pursue their degree.

Maintaining a positive attitude throughout your sonography training program can help keep you from being overwhelmed by the workload. Practice efficient time management skills and maintain good study habits. Balancing your school and personal life can be challenging, but make sure that you set aside some time for leisure activities so that you don't become burned out.

Enhancing Your Qualifications

The prospect of finding a first job after completing an educational program can be daunting. As you complete your educational requirements, consider seeking out a mentor who can help guide you as you embark on your career. You might find a mentor at your school—a teacher or an adviser—or at a health care facility during one of your clinical rotations. A mentor is an experienced professional, usually in the field in which you plan to work, who can listen to your concerns and share expertise. He or she can offer practical tips on the day-to-day duties of a sonographer or career advice, such as how to make a good first impression at a first job.

Employers often require that sonographers hold professional certification, and experienced sonographers recommend that students take the certification exam as soon as possible after graduation. Certification also involves prerequisites such as a certificate or degree from

A mentor's support can give a student confidence in navigating career choices—a mentor can offer personal and career guidance based on experience in the profession.

an accredited program and a certain amount of clinical experience, which is generally completed during training.

Many sonographers apply for the registered diagnostic medical sonographer (RDMS) credential, awarded by ARDMS. There are two test components. Every candidate must pass a Sonography Principles and Instrumentation (SPI) exam. A candidate must also pass one specialty exam out of six options: abdomen, breast, fetal echocardiography, obstetrics and gynecology, or pediatric sonography. ARDMS also offers the Registered Diagnostic Cardiac Sonographer (RDCS), the Registered Vascular Technologist (RVT), and the Registered Musculoskeletal Sonographer (RMSK) credentials. Candidates must pass the SPI exam and an exam in their specialty. Cardiac sonographers take the adult, fetal, or pediatric echocardiography exam.

Two other certifying organizations also offer ultrasound credentials. Cardiovascular Crediting International (CCI), which certifies cardiovascular professionals, offers various certifications in cardiac sonography and vascular technology. The American Registry of Radiologic Technologists (ARRT), which certifies professionals in areas such as medical imaging, offers three sonography credentials: sonography, breast sonography, and vascular sonography.

A few states also have licensing requirements for sonographers. Check to see whether you need to obtain a license to practice sonography in your state.

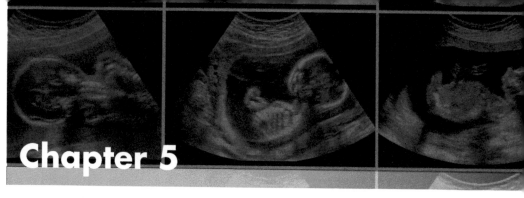

Chapter 5

LANDING THE JOB

Hunting for your first job might seem like a daunting prospect. While you're in the process of completing your sonography program, you may feel like you don't have the time and energy to think about a job search. Nonetheless, you should begin laying the groundwork for your job hunt when you're still in school. Identify your preferred type of workplace, research potential employers in your area, and start making a list of people who could give you a job reference.

Once you've begun your job search, you should be organized and persistent. Keep records of attractive job openings and positions you've applied for—don't stop sending out applications while you're waiting for responses. Set goals and keep a to-do list for your job hunt. If you spend time every day fine-tuning, updating, and expanding your search, you should have no problem finding your first job in sonography.

Researching the job market and looking for potential opportunities early on can help a job seeker plan out job search strategies and map long-term career goals.

Career Resources

As you begin hunting for your first job, take advantage of free and low-cost resources that can help you identify job openings, improve your job application materials, and make a good first impression on prospective employers. The career resource center at your school can be a great aid in finding a first job, and you should familiarize yourself with the services it offers early on during your job search. You'll be able to

Health care job fairs offer students and experienced health care professionals alike an opportunity to talk to recruiters and apply for jobs in the field.

browse sonography job listings and learn about employers in the area. The center also will provide services such as résumé critiques and mock job interviews with career coaches.

Your teachers and classmates may be able to share information on job openings in the field as well. Be sure to ask former professors, advisers, and clinical rotation supervisors for letters of recommendation, and check whether they would be willing to serve as a reference on job applications.

BUILDING A RÉSUMÉ

You should include a résumé and cover letter in every job application. Start building your résumé while you're still in school and update it regularly.

A résumé is a document that summarizes your professional qualifications. All résumés include contact information and sections on education and work experience. You can also include sections on activities, awards, credentials, interests, skills, or volunteer service that might be relevant to sonography and health care. Some résumés include an objective at the beginning and references at the end. There are several different formats for résumés—the "functional" format that highlights abilities and achievements might be a good choice for a new sonographer. Some online career learning centers such as that on UltrasoundJOBS.com or career development sites such as LiveCareer.com offer guidance in putting together a résumé and writing compelling cover letters.

When applying for a job, you should customize your résumé to emphasize skills and achievements applicable to that position. Include keywords pertinent to the job description that will grab the employer's attention. **Pay attention to any specific submission requirements in the job description.**

The cover letter is another important element of a job application, and you should include one unless the job description states, "no cover letters." Your cover letter gives you a chance to introduce yourself and make the case that you're a great candidate for the job. An effective cover letter can grab your prospective employer's attention and make you stand out from the rest of the applicants.

Health care career fairs give students the chance to meet with representatives from a variety of employers. When you attend, dress professionally and take along copies of your résumé to distribute.

Some public libraries also provide career resources and services. You can check out health career guides, books offering general career advice, and newspapers and periodicals with job listings. Libraries may offer employment assistance such as online career tools on library computers, career counseling, or informational sessions with career experts.

Many job seekers use the internet as their primary source of information and job listings. General career sites such as Monster.com and Careerbuilder.com have subsections devoted to health care. There are health care specific career sites, too. Sonographers can read job listings and post a résumé at UltrasoundJOBS.com, which is the official career website of ARDMS.

Keep track of employers in your area who may be hiring. Most big health care facilities have a job opportunities section on their websites. If you hope to find a position with a specific employer, take the initiative to send a résumé to their human resources department. They may keep your résumé on file and contact you when they do have job openings.

Using Your Network

Professional networking can be invaluable for landing your first job and advancing your sonography career. As you start out, your network will consist of family, friends, and peers. Gradually, as you complete clinical rotations and make contacts through school, your network will expand to include various types of health care professionals. Keep in touch with the people in your network, even if it's just an occasional email exchange to catch up with their professional activities. When you're ready to look for a job, let these people know. They might be able to make introductions or offer tips about open positions. When someone in your network is looking for new opportunities, you can help that person out. Networking is all about mutual support.

If you're new to the job market, you may not know that many job openings are filled without ever being listed. You might be able to find out about some such jobs through your network of contacts from clinical rotations or your training program.

As you embark on your career path, keep in touch with your colleagues in the field who make up your professional network.

Joining ARDMS and other professional organizations—such as the American Institute of Ultrasound in Medicine (AIUM), the Society for Vascular Ultrasound (SVU), or the American Society of Echocardiography (ASE)—can increase your circle of contacts in the field. If you have the opportunity to attend health care industry events, don't be shy about introducing yourself to new people. Consider participating in volunteer activities related to health care, where you might have an opportunity to meet fellow professionals in health care fields.

Online social networking sites can serve as a resource in advancing your career. Business and professional networking platforms offer opportunities for online interactions with colleagues. Personal social networks can also be convenient for keeping up connections with health care colleagues.

Be aware of your digital footprint—the impression created by your online activities. Employers often check the social media presence and online activities of job candidates. Your social media profile can be a valuable asset if it emphasizes your personal and professional achievements and demonstrates a solid work ethic. Use privacy settings to restrict access to personal posts and photos to family and friends.

Acing the Interview

If a prospective employer is impressed by your application, the next step is the job interview. Companies sometimes screen applicants during an initial phone interview. The in-person interview at the workplace, however, is your opportunity to sell yourself and convince the employer that you're the ideal candidate for the job.

You should prepare thoroughly for the interview ahead of time. Reread the job description and gather some background information about the workplace. Make a list of questions you have about matters such as working conditions, job expectations, or benefits. Interviewers often ask job applicants to say a few words about themselves or to describe their career goals. Research typical job interview questions that you might expect and prepare some answers ahead of time. Keep your answers professional in tone and emphasize your qualifications and experience.

Make sure you have a good night's sleep the night before your interview and plan to arrive at least fifteen minutes early for the appointment. Dress professionally—business suits are appropriate for both men and women, although women may opt for a blouse and perhaps a blazer with slacks or a skirt. Clothes that are too casual might give the impression that you don't take the interview seriously.

You should project a positive, confident attitude during the interview. Speak clearly, smile, and be aware of your

During a job interview, employers look for candidates who demonstrate that they are positive, capable, and motivated to do their best at the position.

body language—no slouching or fidgeting. Emphasize your willingness to work hard and learn at your first sonography job. Don't make any negative comments about previous employers or your training program.

After the interview, follow up by sending a thank-you note or email. Remind the interviewer that you think you're a great match for the job and that you're excited at the prospect of working at the facility. If you don't hear back within a week, contact the employer to ask about the status of the opening. If you do not get the job, don't be discouraged—determination and perseverance are key to getting a great job offer in the end.

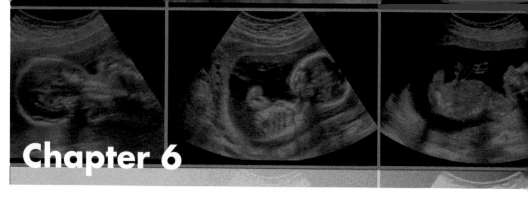

Chapter 6

MAPPING YOUR CAREER PATH

Landing your new job can be exciting and overwhelming. A first job represents the culmination of your education and training, but it also serves as a fresh starting point on your career path. Even as you celebrate your success, you may be asking yourself where you go next in terms of your career arc.

Sonographers often start out working in clinical settings, such as hospitals. Many sonographers are happy spending their entire careers at hospitals, while others move on to different types of health care workplaces. A sonographer may find that he or she prefers working in a setting that presents a variety of cases. On the other hand, another sonographer might develop a preference for a specific type of imaging, such as echocardiography. Set short-term and long-term career goals as you start out but remain flexible and open to new opportunities. You'll benefit from taking advantage of chances to learn on the job and expand your skill set.

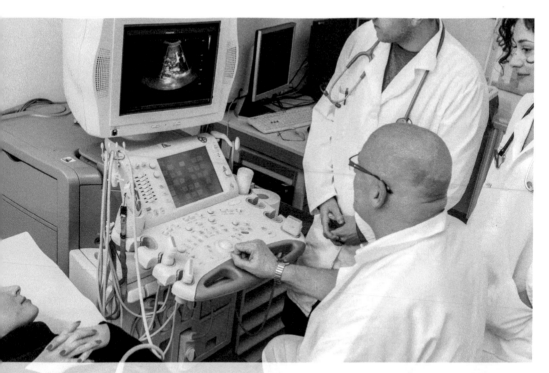

A first job is an opportunity to establish a solid work ethic and learn to work as part of a team of health care professionals in a variety of specialties.

Making a Good Impression

As you begin your career, you should keep a mental tally of the factors that make someone an exceptional sonographer and strive to meet those standards. You should start your new job by establishing yourself as a motivated and reliable employee.

No matter how familiar you are with the sonography workplace from your clinical rotations, you'll have to learn new routines and job responsibilities when you start out.

Your first day will probably include a period of orientation and training, and you'll meet your coworkers, supervisors, and your first patients. Be sure to ask any questions you have about the expectations of your new position or about the terms of employment, such as benefits.

Starting a new job can be overwhelming, and it might take a little while before you feel fully established. You should maintain a positive attitude and approach the position with a willingness to learn from the experience of the people around you. Accept constructive criticism gracefully, and when you receive formal feedback, such as a job performance review, take heed of ways that you can improve your performance.

Sonographers must bring a blend of skills to the job. A sonographer must be confident in making independent decisions and exhibiting leadership, but he or she must also coordinate well with other medical professionals. Intuition can help a sonographer relate well with patients, but problem solving and critical thinking are

Health care workers can be subject to job stress and burnout. Establish effective stress management strategies early on to maintain good health and a positive outlook.

essential to obtaining high-quality images necessary for a sound diagnosis. You might feel a sense of urgency about keeping up with all of your responsibilities, but a principal trait in a sonographer is patience, whether dealing with patients, their family members, colleagues, or administrators.

Sonography can be a demanding field, and you should take positive steps to maintain a sense of balance in your life to avoid overwork and stress. If you find yourself under a lot of stress, learn healthy ways to deal with it during your time off. Eat a balanced diet, get plenty of sleep and exercise, and pursue hobbies and other leisure activities that you enjoy. Take care of your physical well-being, too. Use recommended precautions for avoiding on-the-job injuries, and if you are injured, report it and seek medical help.

Continuing Education and Advancement

As you gain job experience, identify your strengths and interests in planning your next career move. Although sonography is a field with a highly specialized set of skills, this circumstance does not mean that a sonographer is trapped in the same type of position for the course of his or her entire career. Sonographers are needed in a variety of different health care settings, and a sonographer can obtain further education and training that expand available career options.

A sure means of improving employment opportunities is to gain certification in more specialties. Entry-level sonographers take a single specialty exam for their RDMS certification, but as you continue your career, you can study,

INTERVIEW WITH TOM WHELAN

Tom Whelan has been a sonographer for almost thirty-five years. Writer Michelle Brunet interviewed Whelan about the sonography profession for UltrasoundSchoolsInfo.com. His answers to two of Brunet's questions are as follows:

To you, what makes a good sonographer?
Personality-wise you've got to be a people lover, because every time you are dealing with a patient, you're dealing with people who are not having a good day. So you have to empathize with the patient and treat them with respect. That's number one.

Any final words?
To prospective students, take a good hard look at ultrasound. It's not going away. It's going to be a profession that just increases. It's a very rewarding profession. It's also very technical, there is a steep learning curve to it and it takes lifetime dedication. You're never going to know everything about ultrasound because it's constantly changing. Every time you turn around, somebody invents a new procedure that's

(continued on the next page)

(continued from the previous page)

saving people's lives. You have to continue educating yourself. In my humble opinion it would be a wise choice for any person thinking about getting into health care to choose ultrasound as a profession.

gain experience, and take exams in more sonography specialties. Some sonographers choose to pursue certification from more than one certification organization as well.

Certifying organizations require regular renewal of certification. To keep certification current, a sonographer must complete a certain number of continuing medical education (CME) credits. Courses tend to focus on cutting-edge topics in various sonography specialties. They are offered through professional organizations such as ARDMS, AIUM, or the Society of Diagnostic Medical Sonographers (SDMS), as well as by many different medical education providers. Some of these courses may be provided for free for members or a sonographer's employer may pay for them.

Sonography is a high-tech field that is expanding as instruments become more advanced and doctors find more applications for the noninvasive procedure. CMEs provide sonographers with the means of keeping up to date in the field. Sonographers can also read about new breakthroughs and research in publications such as the *Journal of Diagnostic Medical Sonographers*, issued by SDMS, or the *Journal of Ultrasound in Medicine*, issued by AIUM.

New advances in ultrasound technology require that sonographers stay up to date with the latest innovations. Here, ultrasound imaging is used during a robot-assisted prostrate cancer operation.

Conferences and workshops can provide sonographers with opportunities to learn about the latest developments in sonography as well as to network with other professionals. Networking is as important for experienced sonographers as it is for newcomers to the field. Professional organizations can offer great networking opportunities. Online groups and social media connections can provide sonographers with the means of connecting on the internet. The most basic networking strategy, however, is keeping in touch with your circle of colleagues in the field, past and present, as your career progresses. They may let you know if they hear of professional opportunities that might interest you, and you can reciprocate.

Work experience and ongoing education can expand a sonographer's employment opportunities. A sonographer may choose to pursue supervisory or administrative roles, taking on more responsibility for making decisions in the department. Some sonographers go on to train new sonographers in a health care setting or become teachers in educational programs. Experienced sonographers may find work in research, exploring innovative breakthroughs in sonography or making new discoveries using ultrasound imaging in collaboration with scientists in other disciplines. Regardless of a sonographer's specific career focus, sonography is a rewarding field that provides a secure income and gives sonographers the satisfaction of knowing that their work makes a real difference in people's lives.

GLOSSARY

abnormality Something that is different from what is normal, often in a way that indicates that something may be wrong.

anatomy The scientific study dealing with the physical structures of the human body and of other living things.

associate's degree An undergraduate degree generally awarded after two years of study.

bachelor's degree The undergraduate degree awarded after completing a four-year college program.

certification The awarding of a certificate or license upon completion of a course of study or passing of an exam.

clinical Pertaining to the direct treatment and observation of patients.

credential Proof, usually written, that demonstrates someone's identity, authority, or qualifications.

diagnose To identify the nature of a medical condition by examining the symptoms.

echocardiography The use of sonography to image the action of the heart.

fetus An unborn developing baby more than eight weeks old.

ionizing radiation Particles, X-rays, or gamma rays that carry enough energy to ionize or strip electrons from an atom.

license Official permission from the government or other authority, such as to practice a trade.

musculoskeletal Pertaining to the muscles and to the skeleton.

network To maintain communication with a group of people, especially to exchange information about professional opportunities.

qualification The ability to perform a task or fulfill a position; also, formal attainment of certain conditions, such as to hold a position or exercise certain rights.

reference Someone providing a statement of professional qualifications; also, the statement itself.

résumé A summary of one's professional qualifications and work experience.

sonographer A health care professional who uses ultrasound equipment.

stress Strain or tension, involving mental, emotional, and physical responses.

technologist Someone trained in practical application and knowledge in a field of technology.

ultrasound A medical procedure in which high-frequency sound waves are used to image organs and structures of the body.

vascular Relating to the blood vessels of the body.

volunteer To participate in unpaid work.

FOR MORE INFORMATION

American Institute of Ultrasound in Medicine (AIUM)
14750 Sweitzer Lane, Suite 100
Laurel, MD 20707
(301) 498-4100
Website: http://www.aium.org
Facebook, Twitter, and Instagram: @AIUMultrasound
The American Institute of Ultrasound in Medicine promotes
the use of ultrasound and provides educational
resources to its multidisciplinary membership.

American Registry for Diagnostic Medical Sonography
(ARDMS)
1401 Rockville Pike, Suite 600
Rockville, MD 20852-1402
(301) 738-8401
Website: http://www.ardms.org
Facebook and Twitter: @TheARDMS
The American Registry for Diagnostic Medical
Sonography is the certifying organization that awards
ultrasound credentials.

American Registry of Radiologic Technologists (ARRT)
1255 Northland Drive
St. Paul, MN 55120-1155
(651) 687-0048
Website: https://www.arrt.org
Facebook: @americanregistryofradiologictechnologists
The American Registry of Radiologic Technologists is a
certifying organization that awards credentials in
medical imaging, interventional procedures, and
radiation therapy.

American Society of Echocardiography (ASE)
2530 Meridian Parkway, Suite 450
Durham, NC 27713
(919) 861-5574
Website: http://asecho.org
Facebook: @asecho
Twitter: @ASE360
The American Society of Echocardiography is a professional organization promoting cardiovascular ultrasound and providing educational resources to its membership.

Bureau of Labor Statistics (BLS)
US Department of Labor
2 Massachusetts Avenue NE, Suite 2135
Washington, DC 20212-0001
(202) 691-5700
Website: http://www.bls.gov
This federal agency analyzes the labor market activity, industry working conditions, and price changes in the US economy. Every year, the BLS updates the Occupational Outlook Handbook (https://www.bls.gov/ooh), which describes thousands of careers, including those in sonography and ultrasound, with details about job requirements and average salaries.

Cardiovascular Credentialing International (CCI)
1500 Sunday Drive, Suite 102
Raleigh, NC 27607
(919) 861-4539
Website: http://www.cci-online.org
Cardiovascular Credentialing International is the certifying

organization that awards cardiovascular technology credentials.

Health Canada
Address Locator 0900C2
Ottawa, ON K1A 0K9
Canada
(613) 957-2991
Website: https://www.canada.ca/en/health-canada
.html
Facebook: @HealthyCdns, @HealthyFirstNationsandInuit
Twitter: @GovCanHealth
Health Canada is Canada's national department of
health. The department's website includes information
on medical sonography.

Society for Vascular Ultrasound (SVU)
4601 Presidents Drive, Suite 260
Lanham, MD 20706-4831
(301) 459-7550
Website: http://www.svunet.org
Facebook: @SocietyforVascularUltrasound
Twitter: @svuinfo
The Society for Vascular Ultrasound is a professional
organization promoting noninvasive technology used
to diagnose vascular disease and providing educational resources to its membership.

Society of Diagnostic Medical Sonographers (SDMS)
2745 Dallas Parkway, Suite 350
Plano, TX 75093
(214) 473-8057

Website: https://www.sdms.org
Facebook: @SDMS3
Twitter: @TheSDMS
The Society of Diagnostic Medical Sonographers is a
    professional organization that advances ultrasound
    and educates its membership.

Sonography Canada
PO Box 1220
Kemptville, ON K0G 1J0
Canada
(613) 258-0855
Website: http://www.sonographycanada.ca
Facebook: @SonographyCanada
Sonography Canada is the certifying organization that
    awards ultrasound credentials in Canada.

FOR FURTHER READING

Angulo, Roberto. *Getting Your First Job*. Hoboken, NJ: John Wiley & Sons, Inc., 2018.

Ferguson. *Encyclopedia of Careers and Vocational Guidance*. 17th ed. New York, NY: Ferguson, 2017.

Fry, Ronald W. *101 Great Answers to the Toughest Interview Questions*. Wayne, NJ: Career Press, 2016.

Hubbard, Rita L. *What Degree Do I Need to Pursue a Career in Health Care?* New York, NY: Rosen Publishing, 2015.

Morkes, Andrew. *Hot Health Care Careers: 30 Occupations with Fast Growth and Many New Job Openings*. 2nd ed. Chicago, IL: College & Career Press, 2017.

Reeves, Diane Lindsey. *Health Sciences: Exploring Career Pathways*. Ann Arbor, MI: Cherry Lake Publishing, 2017.

Schwarzenegger, Katherine. *I Just Graduated ... Now What? Honest Answers from Those Who Have Been There*. New York, NY: Crown Archetype, 2014.

Sheen, Barbara. *Careers in Health Care*. San Diego, CA: ReferencePoint Press, Inc., 2015.

Troutman, Kathryn K. *Creating Your First Resume: A Step-by-Step Guide to Write Your First Competitive Resume*. Catonsville, MD: Federal Career Changing Institute, 2016.

Vernon, Naomi. *A Teen's Guide to Finding a Job*. San Antonio, TX: New Beginnings, 2013.

Yate, Martin John. *Knock 'em Dead: The Ultimate Job Search Guide*. New York, NY: Adams Media, 2017.

BIBLIOGRAPHY

American College of Chest Physicians. "X-rays Overused in ICU: Ultrasound Safer, Just as Effective." *ScienceDaily*, October 28, 2013. https://www.sciencedaily.com/releases /2013/10/131028114834.htm.

American Registry for Diagnostic Medical Sonography, Inc. "Sonographer Testimonials." Retrieved March 5, 2018. http://www.ardms.org/Discover-ARDMS /careers-in-sonography/Pages/Sonographer%20 Testimonials.aspx.

Brunet, Michelle. "Interview with Tom Whelan, Sonographer, Teacher and Pioneer (Part 2)." Retrieved March 6, 2018. https://www .ultrasoundschoolsinfo.com/interview-with-tom -whelan-sonographer-teacher-and-pioneer-part-2.

Bureau of Labor Statistics. "Diagnostic Medical Sonographers and Cardiovascular Technologists and Technicians, Including Vascular Technologists." US Department of Labor, *Occupational Outlook Handbook*, January 30, 2018. https://www.bls .gov/ooh/healthcare/diagnostic-medical -sonographers.htm.

Bureau of Labor Statistics. "Labor Force Statistics from the Current Population Survey." January 19, 2018. https://www.bls.gov/cps/cpsaat11.htm.

Enelow, Wendy S., and Louise M. Kursmark. *Expert Resumes for Health Careers*. 2nd ed. Indianapolis, IN: JIST Works, 2010.

Ferguson. *Exploring Health Care Careers*. 3rd ed. New York, NY: Ferguson, 2006.

Ferguson. *What Can I Do Now? Health Care*. New York, NY: Ferguson, 2007.

Field, Shelly. *Career Opportunities in Health Care*. 3rd
    ed. New York, NY: Checkmark Books, 2007.
Moyer, Sarah. "How to Get Started in Ophthalmic
    Imaging." Ophthalmic Photographers Society.
    Retrieved February 2018. http://www.opsweb
    .org/?page=CareerPathways.
Murphey, Susan. "Work Related Musculoskeletal
    Disorders and Sonography." Excerpted white paper.
    Society of Diagnostic Medical Sonography.
    Retrieved March 6, 2018. http://www.sdms.org
    /resources/careers/work-related-musculoskeletal
    -disorders.
National Institute of Biomedical Imaging and
    Bioengineering. "Ultrasound." July 2016. https://
    www.nibib.nih.gov/science-education/science
    -topics/ultrasound.
O*NET OnLine. "Summary Report for: 29-2032.00—
    Diagnostic Medical Sonographers." Retrieved
    March 5, 2018. https://www.onetonline.org
    /link/summary/29-2032.00.
Quan, Kathy. *The Everything Guide to Careers in
    Health Care: Find the Job That's Right for You*. Avon,
    MA: Adams Media, 2007.
Radiological Society of North America, Inc. (RSNA).
    "RadiologyInfo.org for Patients." Retrieved March 6,
    2018. https://www.radiologyinfo.org.
Society of Diagnostic Medical Sonography.
    "Understanding Sonography." Retrieved March 5,
    2018. http://www.sdms.org/resources/what-is
    -sonography/understanding-sonography.
"Ultrasound Technician Center." Retrieved February 26,
    2018. https://www.ultrasoundtechniciancenter.org.

US Food and Drug Administration. "Ultrasound Imaging." December 4, 2017. https://www.fda .gov/Radiation-EmittingProducts /RadiationEmittingProductsandProcedures /MedicalImaging/ucm115357.htm.

Wischnitzer, Saul, and Edith Wischnitzer. *Top 100 Health-Care Careers: Your Complete Guidebook to Training and Jobs in Allied Health, Nursing, Medicine, and More.* 3rd ed. Indianapolis, IN: JIST Works, 2011.

INDEX

About the Author

Corona Brezina is an author who has written numerous young adult books. Several of her previous works have also focused on high-tech and in-demand careers, including *Careers in Digital Media; Careers in Nanotechnology; Getting a Job in Health Care; Careers as a Medical Examiner;* and *Top STEM Careers in Math.* She lives in Chicago, Illinois.

Photo Credits

Cover (figure) Mangostock/Shutterstock.com; cover (background) sfam_photo/Shutterstock.com; back cover, p. 1 (background graphic) HunThomas/Shutterstock.com; pp. 4–5 (background) and interior pages GagliardiImages/Shutterstock.com; p. 5 Hero Images/Getty Images; p. 8 Victor Habbick Visions/Science Photo Library/Getty Images; p. 9 Philippe Roy/Cultura/Getty Images; p. 11 Burger Phanie/Canopy/Getty Images; pp. 17, 51 Bloomberg/Getty Images; p. 21 Andresr/E+/Getty Images; pp. 23, 37 BSIP/Universal Images Group/Getty Images; p. 26 GagliardiImages/Shutterstock .com; p. 28 © iStockphoto.com/Simpson33; p. 30 Monty Rakusen /Cultura/Getty Images; p. 31 SABarton/E+/Getty Images; p. 34 Alexander Tsiaras/Science Source; p. 40 Adam Crowley/Blend Images/Getty Images; p. 41 Simon Jarratt/Corbis/VCG/Getty Images; p. 44 Andy Cross/Denver Post/Getty Images; p. 47 Monkey Business Images/Shutterstock.com; pp. 50, 55 Rawpixel.com/ Shutterstock.com; p. 57 Africa Studio/Shutterstock.com; p. 60 Choja /E+/Getty Images; p. 61 Lucky Business/Shutterstock.com; p. 65 Jeff Pachoud/AFP/Getty Images.

Design: Michael Moy; Layout: Ellina Litmanovich; Senior Editor: Kathy Kuhtz Campbell; Photo Researcher: Sherri Jackson